D0969129

The Standard Publishing Company, Cincinnati, Ohio.
A division of Standex International Corporation.
© 1992 by The Standard Publishing Company
Printed in the United States of America
99 98 97 96 95 94 93 92   5 4 3 2 1

Library of Congress Cataloging-in-Publication Data
Odor, Ruth Shannon, 1926-
The very special visitors : the story of the Wise Men /
retold by Ruth Shannon Odor ; illustrated by Karen Clark.
ISBN 0-87403-955-X
Library of Congress Catalog Card Number 91-46807

The Very Special Visitors

The story of the wise men retold by
Ruth Shannon Odor

illustrated by
Karen Clark

STANDARD
PUBLISHING

"A star will come out of Jacob;
a scepter will rise out of Israel."

Numbers 24:17
New International Version

Visitors often come to our homes.
Who comes to visit you?

Sometimes the visitors are Grandma and Grandpa,
or your aunt and uncle,
or your next-door neighbor.
Sometimes the visitors are boys and girls
who come to play with you.

The Bible tells about some very special visitors
who came to see Jesus when He was a child.

These visitors were wise and wealthy men
who lived in a faraway eastern land.
They studied the stars.
They studied writings too.

One night they saw a new star in the sky.

"Look!" said the wise
and wealthy men.
"A new star,
bright and shining!
It must be the star of the
child born to be king!"

"We must visit this child,"
said the wise and wealthy men.
"We will take Him presents—
gold and frankincense and myrrh.
We will ride on our camels.
It will be a long, long trip."

So they got their camels ready.

They packed the presents
they would give to the child—
gold and frankincense and myrrh.

They said good-bye to their friends.

Now they were the very special visitors,
on their way to see the child born to be king!

For days and days, they rode on their camels
over the desert sand.
They were hot and dusty and tired,
but, oh, how much they wanted to see the child!

At last they came to the city of Jerusalem.
"Where is the child born to be king?" they asked.
"We saw His star in the east,
and we have come to worship Him."

"Go to Bethlehem," they were told.
"It is written that Bethlehem is the place He will be born."

On toward Bethlehem rode the very special visitors.
They looked up in the sky,
and there was the star they had seen back home!
They followed the star until it stopped,
right over a house in Bethlehem!

The very special visitors knocked on the door.

A man came to the door.
"We have come to see the child
born to be king," said the visitors.
"We saw His star in the east,
and we have come to worship Him."

"Then do come in,"
said the man at the door.

The man was Joseph.
Inside the house were Mary
and little Jesus—
the child the very special visitors
had come so far to see.

They bowed down before Him.
They gave Him their presents—
gold and frankincense and myrrh.

When the very special visitors were ready to leave,
they said good-bye to Mary and Joseph and Jesus.

They climbed up on their camels
and began the long trip home.

They talked about Bethlehem
and the bright, shining star.
They talked about Jesus,
the child born to be king.

How glad they were
that they had been His very special visitors!